Live an
Amazing Life

Laurie,
Thanks for your
Support! Keep

Robyn Beazley

dreaming big &
smiling. Live Inspired,

Robyn

Library and Archives Canada Cataloguing in Publication

Beazley, Robyn
    Live an amazing life: stories that encourage and inspire positive attitude / Robyn Beazley.
    1st. pbk. ed.

Includes bibliographic references.
ISBN 978–0–9867147–0–2

The article entitled Why We Dream(board) Together on pages 64-69 of this book is printed by permission of its coauthor John Beazley.

Technical Credits:
    Primary editor: *Megan Shapka*
    Secondary editors: *Randi Pierce, Tiffany Dowell, John Beazley, Sheree Obbagy, Sandra Mills*
    Cover Design: *Concept International Design*
    Interior Design & Layout: *T.L. Price Freelance*
    Back cover text: *Megan Shapka*
    Back cover image of author: *Lori Loree – Loree Photography*

Printed in Canada by *Blitzprint Inc,* Calgary, Alberta

The purpose of this book is to educate and entertain. The author and/or publisher do not guarantee that anyone following these techniques, suggestions, tips, idea, or strategies will become successful. The author and/or publisher shall have neither liability nor responsibility to anyone with respect to any loss or damage caused, or alleged to be caused, directly or indirectly by the information contained in this book.

For more information about our products and services, visit: www.robynbeazley.com

• • •

*To my amazing husband, John,
who inspires me every day and
loves me unconditionally.*

• • •

Contents

Contents

Hello, Nice to Meet You

• • •

I dare you to make someone smile or laugh.

~ Robyn Beazley

• • •

You may associate an amazing life with monetary or materialistic wealth, but I'm going to challenge your way of thinking. My goal is to help you *Live an Amazing Life* by finding the optimistic, positive side of life and the beauty in everything around you.

Right off the bat, I'll admit that I am far from perfect. I'm human - and I make mistakes. I learn to do by doing (4-H motto). I spend money when I don't have it to spend, (I'm a woman. I love shiny, blingy items and I'm drawn to sale signs like a bug to a light). I personally struggle with many fears; rejection and concern that my friends feel I'm too pushy are just a few of them.

I'm not a celebrity, millionaire, or superstar - *yet*. I'm just like many of you – an ordinary girl living the (North) "American Dream." I have a husband with an exciting career, a well-decorated house, a nice car, a lot of aspirations, and debt! I'm on a quest to make my first million and recently heard that it will cost me a million to get there. So, I'm right on track.

Throughout this book, I share my personal experiences and recipe for living a full, abundant life. My formula has been developed from the experience and wisdom I have gained from my amazing network. (I'm a huge copycat – the best copycat wins, right?) I believe that when you learn as much as you can from other people's success, you will succeed!

You may have heard some of these principles before, but my goal is to present at least one idea in a unique way that will resonate with you and reignite your passions.

Growing up on a ranch in Alberta, Canada my parents taught me and my two siblings the value of hard work – and the rewards that followed. My parents blessed me with many opportunities to grow as a woman and provided me with a solid foundation for positive attitude.

By choosing to be happy, I make the most of every day. I attribute my ability to tackle life and attract everything I've ever needed and wanted, to my positive attitude. I hope that you identify with some of these stories throughout this book and may they empower you to share your own experiences to help others.

Now that I've introduced myself, I'd like to thank you for the chance to discover life together.

Life is a blessing – receive it, cherish it, pass it on. Every day I overcome the naysayers and negative emotions that surround all of us, with a smile and God by my side. We are all given the gift of life and the opportunity to create the journey we want. It's our choice to overcome the challenges that we all face.

Are you willing to start thinking differently and let today be the first day of the rest of your life? Then sit down and buckle up for the ride!

Attitude

...

Attitude is a little thing that makes a big difference.

~ Winston Churchill

...

What Doesn't Kill You Makes You Stronger

Just over one year ago, my fantastic network blessed me with three speaking engagements to share my passion for life with their audiences.

Luckily, I had been in 4-H for eight years and learned the basic skills of public speaking. My time spent competing on a collegiate livestock judging team, while getting my degree, helped me develop my ability to speak further. At the time I committed to these awesome speaking engagements, I wanted to sharpen my skills. John and I talked about getting involved with Toastmasters, so I started looking into local chapters.

I attended my first fact seeking meeting alone and even published a blog post about getting involved with this fabulous organization.

The following week, my husband was back in town and attended with me. After the meeting, we looked at the information package and I was ready to sign the membership form. However, my budget officer of a husband vetoed the idea due to our lack of finances. (I had just started a new job, but was in catch up mode from six months of job searching and lack of cash flow.)

I was crushed. I was also embarrassed. I learned that one of the ladies from the Toastmasters chapter worked at the same place where I had just begun my new job. When we passed in the hall for the first time she asked, "Why haven't you joined?" Another more "experienced" lady from our church (who I did not recognize at the meeting or at church that Sunday) came up to me after a service and questioned, "Why didn't you come back?" I chose to hide my tears and attempt to protect my pride by replying, "We aren't able to join right now." The truth was that we couldn't afford to attend and the truth hurt.

It is a dream of mine that one day, I will be an anonymous person that blesses people with memberships to organizations like Toastmasters, or provides anonymous donations for personal growth opportunities. I absolutely did not expect someone to do that for us, I simply want to have the financial freedom to bless others with such a gift.

Realizing that what doesn't kill you makes you stronger, I jumped over this obstacle and looked for different ways to get prepared for my presentations. I was a sponge, even more than usual. I watched as many speakers as I could for the next few months and watched many YouTube clips; two particular live opportunities stick out in my mind.

One opportunity developed at the college where I've been blessed to contract my services for over a year. I was sitting in my office on a Friday morning when a coworker emailed and asked if I was going to the presentation. I replied, "What presentation?"

"Oh the one in the theater...it's something motivating." I had no idea about this opportunity. I looked at my clock and realized it was beginning in seven minutes! Since I'm flexible and was up for a little break, I decided I could finish the project at hand later.

I went to the theater with no knowledge of what the presentation was about or who was speaking. I walked in, and on each desk, sat a workbook.

I still hadn't clued in to the authors name. I looked around and could see the speaker sitting down in the front row waiting to begin. Then the speaker was introduced: Dr. Joseph Michelli, PhD, author of the book, *The Starbucks Experience*. I was really excited, as I had just read his book while on vacation the month before.

Dr. Michelli's speech was fabulous. The way he gave his presentation resonated with me even more than the content. I observed how he interacted with the audience, varied his voice, asked questions, and presented himself. I was inspired. I was only seven days away from launching my own speaking career. At the end of the presentation, I asked to take a photo with Dr. Michelli. {View the picture on my blog at www.robynbeazley.com.}

When you least expect it, the exact opportunities you need present themselves. It is said that the only difference between today and five years from today are the people you meet and books you read. The people and experiences in our life shape us, not the material things. I didn't have to attend this presentation or change my plan. However, I am thankful that I did. When you stop learning, you stop living.

The second opportunity came through a network marketing business national conference. Michael "Pinball" Clemons, a retired Canadian football player, spoke right to my heart that day. I videotaped a few segments of his presentation on my digital camera and watched them over and over. I was focusing on Pinball's body language, voice fluctuation, and how successfully he engaged the audience. He demonstrated that no matter who is in the audience, you could make everyone feel like you are talking right to them.

You can't control every situation but you can control how you respond to every situation.

Bite Your Tongue

A year and a half ago a job posting for an agriculture company caught my eye. I always wanted to work for them, so, I applied. I talked to a couple of individuals in my network that worked or had worked for them in hopes of gaining a personal referral or two.

I felt like I soared through my phone interview, as I was immediately requested to schedule an in-person interview.

Here's a brief synopsis of what was going on in my life at the time. I had just finished producing an event that lost a lot of money, or large investment into the business (whichever way you would like to look at it). It boiled down to needing a real J.O.B. (Just Over Broke) immediately, to make ends meet.

As I prepared the day before my interview, I realized that the only classy outfit I had, and most importantly that fit, was a dark brown skirt suit. (I would have preferred to wear a pant suit). After my costly business endeavor just a month earlier, I had overeaten in an attempt to drown my sorrows. I had eaten myself into a bigger me and had no money to buy new interview clothes.

When I went to get my conservative high heels the morning of the interview, I realized they were missing in action. Now, if I had mentioned this obstacle to any of my family members, they would have laughed and commented on how I'm always losing things. The truth is, I don't often lose items – I just temporarily misplace them.

I went digging in my giveaway box for a pair of brown shoes. My options were a pair of dirty, ugly loafers or a pair of hard to walk in, backless high heels. For whatever reason, I decided on the heels. Remember, this interview was for an agriculture sales position, so I did not make a very realistic footwear choice.

During my interview, I recall using the words "amazing" and "diva" when answering their questions, only to bite my tongue hard both times. I quickly realized these bubbly words weren't suitable when interviewing for an agriculture position, whose clients would be primarily male. I didn't say them on purpose; I was just being me!

To this day, I would love to know the reason why I wasn't further considered for the position. After two interviews, the biggest disappointment came when all I received was a generic "thanks for your time" corporate email. I kept wondering why a company wouldn't want a fireball like me working for them. Was it the outfit or the two outrageous, flowery words? I later discovered that I had left my conservative brown shoes at a friend's house after volunteering for a charity event. Honestly, I doubt the shoes were the turning point!

I concluded the company missed out and I don't regret anything. Still, there is a part of me that wants to take two copies of this book, highlight this section and mark this page with a note saying, "Read this part" and send a copy to each manager that interviewed me! However, I'm bigger than that...I think.

This experience reinforced my belief that everything happens for a reason.

Release Negative Energy

When I'm frustrated or angry – I write. I write down what I'm thinking: the good, the bad, and the ugly; the celebrations and the challenges; my goals, dreams, and desires.

One of the most entertaining visuals of this is when I'm the passenger in the car travelling down the road with my delightful partner, John, and something has ticked me off (it's usually about money). You can be sure that I'm digging in my purse or one of the many bags I have packed for something to write on; the back of an envelope, a sticky note, anything I can get my hands on. I write exactly how I'm feeling.

This is my personal way of releasing all of the negative energy and anger from my soul. It has to leave my body somehow or I may explode! It is my goal to get it out of my system as fast as I can. I've discovered that if this "trash" stays inside my mind, it attempts to conquer my positive attitude.

If I don't get it out of my system, it can eat at my physical body because I look to food for comfort, which makes me feel even worse. I mentally give myself headaches and stomach pains. I truly believe that everything is mental.

After I write it down, I usually destroy the piece of paper by throwing it away, burning it, or flushing it down the toilet. (I don't actually use the toilet it to discard my papers – I just visualize it.)

You may be the kind of person that needs to talk to express your feelings and release the toxic waste that is built up inside of you. If you need to talk instead of write, I suggest you get a recorder and talk into it or simply call your voicemail and leave yourself a message.

If you record yourself, I suggest deleting it once you record it. Do not listen to it. This action step helps you remove any negativity from your system. Everything you're experiencing has to come out of your system through some emotion, whether it be smiling, laughing, yelling, or crying.

It is not the best idea to share your anger and negative energy with your partner, co-worker, or anyone around you in the heat of the moment. Try to remember the duck on the pond, while the surface appears calm and still, underneath his legs are paddling frantically.

I highly recommend not puking your negative thoughts on someone else. I realize sometimes we may choose to call a close friend, as that's what true friends are for. However, you can't use that card all of the time or soon people won't want to be your friend anymore. Use the "puke on a friend" lifeline for really special circumstances.

I encourage you to find a way to release your negative energy fast and efficiently. It will help you move on quickly and get into a more positive frame of mind!

Positive Energy

One of my least favorite words is the "h" word: hate. It's a very cold and negative word. You won't often hear me say it; and please try not to use it around me!

Where am I going with this? One tool I use to keep my energy level as high as I can is to use the term *"don't prefer"* instead of the "h" word. I learned at a very young age that I didn't receive the response I was looking for if I said the "h" word.

For example, I detested tomatoes in their whole form and still do. When I was a kid I would slide them to the side of my plate as discreetly as possible. During one meal, I vividly recall my strict father questioning what I was doing. He would probably say now that he was just testing my character.

I responded, "I hate tomatoes"; to which I was immediately instructed to eat them against my will. I refused and left the dinner table in tears. From that day forward, I started politely saying, "I didn't prefer them," and as far as I can recall, it was never challenged again.

In the last couple years I've also been practicing eliminating "can't" and "try" from my vocabulary. When writing note cards, emails, or on social media, I say, "I look forward to seeing you," instead of saying "I can't wait to see you."

Don't get me wrong – I am a work in progress and always will be. My husband, family, and friends truly know that! I get sick, depressed, and sad; but I always look for the positive light, however small it may be at the time, allowing that optimism to grow and multiply into brilliant energy. It takes work. It doesn't just happen. I have to talk to myself all the time.

As I mentioned earlier, everything is mental. If you feel like you're getting sick and focus on it, then it will happen. You will wake up and focus on the illness, whether it is that scratchy feeling in the back of your throat or the knot in your stomach. The more you think or say out loud "I'm getting sick" or include it in your social media updates, the more you are looking for this negative attention.

When you foolishly think this way, you're saying, "Welcome strep throat, tonsillitis, and sinus infection into my body. Come right on in sickness. I'm going to stay in bed and take the day off."

We have a house rule. You're allowed a 24-hour pity party and that is it. If you're not feeling well or are having a bad day, then one day is all that is allowed. "Get over it" is our motto. In our house, during a 24-hour pity party, you are allowed a single delivery of chicken noodle soup and a grilled cheese sandwich. Then you're done getting special attention!

Typically the encouragement to get over myself comes within minutes instead of a full day. I laugh with John all the time because when he pouts, I question how long it's going to last and his consistent response is "About 10 minutes."

Self-talk always comes into play. I used to say, "Robyn, you are not sick," until I learned that the Universe doesn't hear the negative (the not) – it just hears what you say. So by saying, "I am not sick," all it hears is, "I am sick."

When I'm feeling under the weather I take a hot shower to wake up and shake everything out of my system or I take a bath before bed to unwind and warm up. I curl up in my flannel PJs to balance my body temperature. It seems that most of the time illness attempts to attack my system right after an intense, stressful event.

I have done lots of event planning in my short life, and absolutely love the rush of flying around to make sure I take care of all of the details. After an event, my immune system is weak from the long days of high stress. I've been working hard the last two years on staying balanced, instead of going through a fluctuation of stress levels.

Another pity party I want to remind you of is the self-inflicted hangover. The longer you baby it, the longer it will last (that's something you may want to consider the next morning that you're feeling sorry for yourself).

What you think about, you bring about!

Bucket Filler or Bucket Dipper?

I love this way of describing an individual's attitude! I first learned about the terms from Victoria Osteen (www.victoriaosteen.com), an amazing pastor, author, and speaker from Houston, Texas. Then I heard a very outgoing, inspirational contestant on a TV game show use the phrase multiple times. Here is my interpretation of "Bucket Filler or Bucket Dipper":

• • •

Are people instantly attracted to you or are you more like mold - and grow on people?

~ Robyn Beazley

• • •

I suggest you be the type of person that has the ability to grace others with your presence. Do you ask questions about other people or do you "puke" your life stories on them when it's uncalled for? Do you add value to other people's lives by sharing positive energy with them?

Can you think of a person in your life who is a downer? Let me help jog your memory. Is there someone in your life whose name, if it popped up on your Caller ID, you likely wouldn't answer it for fear of the ugly attitude or drama on the other end of the phone? As you probably know from personal experience, it can really put a damper on your entire day.

Turn the table around and put yourself in that person's shoes. Do you want to ruin someone else's amazing day?

Think before you call – are you being a drama queen / king? Are you being a bucket dipper? A friend taught me to ask myself, "Can you come up with three solutions to your problem, and one that has to do with you?"

I suggest waiting until you cool down before working through any emotions or discussing it with another person who has a conflicting personality. I encourage you to see the best in every situation and try to find something positive from every situation life throws you.

Once you have taken out the trash and banished your negative mindset. Work through the obstacle with effective communication, either with self-talk or talking to the person directly, to resolve the challenge. When a solution is reached, walk away from the situation. Do not bring up dirty laundry. If you raise the topic (a.k.a. the fight) again, you are the weaker person. Become a strong-minded individual and move on.

When you get off a phone call or are done talking to someone face to face, how do you feel? All warm and fuzzy inside? So excited that you had a chance to talk to that person? Is your body literally vibrating because *you* spoke a lot? Were you talking about yourself the entire time? Based on my experience, we were talking about ourselves when we have this feeling. We all love to talk about ourselves, so remember to ask the other person about things they are interested in also.

Listening to problems, drama, and about other people's excitement gets old really quick! I realize there are days when we all need to vent and get things off of our minds, positive or negative; happy or sad. Just be aware and ask yourself, "Am I bucket dipper or bucket filler?"

Pay it Forward

Whatever you want to receive you must give. It's the "pay it forward" method of blessing the Universe. If you want to receive gorgeous flowers from a special someone, then order or hand-deliver flowers to someone you appreciate. If you want to receive more words of encouragement at work or from your network, then give more encouragement to everyone in your life (including the nice and not so nice people you know). As my friend, Tricia, reminded me recently, "Kill them with kindness." It can be as simple as, "I like your shoes!"

• • •

Be so busy giving recognition
that you don't need it.

~ Jim Rohn

• • •

Get into the selfless mindset and when you least expect it opportunities to pay it forward will jump out in front of you. It is up to you to act on them. One of the most common examples of paying it forward is to buy the coffee for the person in the drive-thru behind you. It is the best gift to give to a person who doesn't know you. You'll most likely never receive a thank you from them and that's the point; giving with no expectations in return.

Following this principle is key to being a successful business person as well. Give referrals to other business owners and entrepreneurs if you wish to receive any in your career. One of my favorite books is *The Go-Giver* by Bob Burg and John David Mann; it's full of examples of selfless acts.

As my friend has experienced:

• • •

I catch myself doing it [paying it forward] without thinking about it anymore!

~ Justine Simpson

• • •

I trust the same thing will happen to you.

While returning to work from lunch one day, I heard a radio advertisement for the new value menu at a fast food joint. It included ice cream treats for $1.49! I thought about the calories in one of these desserts for about one second and then made a quick detour to the restaurant. I returned with eight delightful treats for a few coworkers and myself (of course). It was the best way I could have spent $12.52 that day.

• • •

Buy people ice cream, because ice cream makes people happy!

~ Dave Ritchie

• • •

One day I went to the post office to mail a package and buy stamps. I like to have them on hand to send "just because", birthday, and seasonal cards. The wait was about 15 minutes since there were quite a few people ahead of me. By the time I had been helped, the line was twice as long as it was when I had started.

As I walked past the last two people in line, I overheard a gentleman sweetly tell a woman, "All I'm waiting for is to get a Yankee stamp to send this to my Yankee daughter!"

Immediately I had a flashback of my time living in the United States. My mother was so awesome and sent me a lot of snail mail. I'm sure she phoned, mailed, and emailed me something every day for the first 30 days after I packed up and left the country at 18. She backed off from daily communication after that, but to this day still stays consistent with unique messages.

I giggled (inside) and quickly turned around. Excusing myself for interrupting, I said, "I have a U.S. stamp!"

Before the man could respond, I was reaching for the booklet in my purse. I pulled off a stamp and handed it to him. In shock he said, "How much are they?"

He repeated himself, "Thanks, how much do I owe you?"

I smiled and said, "Nothing! Please pay it forward."

The man responded, "I do every day; doing everything I can for others. I learned that from my mother."

I smiled again and replied, "Have an amazing day!"

As I left, I heard the woman he had commented to, say, "The Christmas spirit has started early."

"Oh honey," I thought, "you're mistaken! I definitely don't give random acts of kindness just around the festive season. I do it all year long, no special occasion necessary. I trust you do the same!"

It is the little things that can make a big difference.

Escape

Everyone needs places and things that take them to their happy zone. A few of mine include baths, wine, candles, beaches, music, pedicures, dancing, sunrises and sunsets.

It's easy to get down and moody. Being a positive person is a full-time job and a lot of work! However, I think it is one of the most rewarding things you can do for yourself and the people around you. Positive energy is contagious!

Make a decision – right now – to only feed yourself positive thoughts. Thoughts lead to actions and actions lead to results. If you want positive results, you need positive thoughts.

Instead of saying, "I'm okay," fake it until you arrive at the emotional place you want to be and exclaim, "I am amazing. How are you beautiful?"

It may be hard for you to believe, but I sometimes have horrible (downright ugly), "ready to go back to bed and start the day over" kind of days. However, I still put a smile on my face and tell myself that God only gives obstacles to those he knows can overcome them. There is always someone you know that has something worse going on in his or her life. What I'm going through isn't the first time someone has gone through this and it won't be the last.

• • •

*Be kinder than necessary, for everyone
you meet is fighting some kind of battle.*

~ Attributed to both
T.H. Thompson and John Watson

• • •

Build up your self-talk! You are strong, gorgeous, talented, and kind. Unleash this positive individual inside you and will begin to touch others with your passion for life.

Surprise and Delight

When you get dressed up and eat a nice dinner with an array of cutlery elegantly spread before you, how does it make you feel?

If you were to make a grilled cheese sandwich, plop it on your everyday dishes, and serve it, how would you feel?

If that same sandwich was served to you on fine china (the fancy type that is being stored in your china cabinet or tucked away in a box), cut in an elegant triangle, served with a pickle, and cloth napkin, how would your perception of that sandwich change?

It's more gourmet, right? You may just sit up a little straighter to eat.

Often when people think of eating an elegant lunch, they think of dining at a high-end bistro or restaurant. They think only wealthier people can afford such luxuries. I say, fake it until you make it!

At Chateau Beazley our friends and family rave about the presentation and service we provide. We aren't professional cooks, maids or butlers; we just love entertaining with flair!

When my husband and I got married, my mother insisted we register for fine china. John and I could appreciate having nice dishes to entertain with, but we weren't interested in tying up a couple hundred dollars per place setting, ultimately, into a china set that may date itself in ten years.

Instead, we bought a box set of china with eight place settings. The dishes are not meant to go through the dishwasher. However, our lifestyle isn't conducive to that, and therefore they go through "Martha." I realize that their lifetime of looking spectacular may be scaled back, but that's okay.

We use our china at least twice a week; if not more. We eat many meals on them, from a casual breakfast for just the two of us to a dinner party of [eight].

It's all about presentation. What are you waiting for – a special occasion? Today is special! You've been blessed with another day on Earth. What is the worst that's going to happen? That they break? They're just plates – start experiencing life with them.

• • •

I love this concept. I have a good friend who is the same way. When we visit her, she serves tea in antique teacups and other beverages, like beer, in crystal glasses. Visitors get scared and ask, "What if I break it?" She says, "It's only crystal!"

~ Megan Shapka

• • •

Amazing Action Steps

- Ask yourself daily whether the glass is half-full or overflowing. Life is what you make it!

- Make light of the little things and have fun.

- Smile - it takes fewer muscles to smile than it does to frown.

- Live in the moment.

- Celebrate everything – little and big. John and I love cracking open a bottle of champagne and toasting, "Here's to Tuesday" (we copied the idea from the movie *Failure to Launch*).

- Live with no regrets. Your experiences shapes who you are.

- Stop and smell the roses no matter the season or location. There is always joy in snow, fall leaves, grass turning green, and seeing a garden grow and flourish with flowers.

- Perform random acts of kindness as often as you can. Pay it forward.

- Plan a meal for yourself or a group of people and serve food using your nice dishes and/or special glasses. Pull out that special outfit you've been saving to wear and plan an evening in or out.

Personal Development

• • •

You are today where your thoughts have brought you; you will be tomorrow where your thoughts take you.

~ James Allen

• • •

Lifelong Learning

I am addicted to personal growth and constantly:

- Read and listen to personal growth books and audio books

- Listen to motivational speakers

- Attend every free workshop/event I can fit into my schedule

- Subscribe to many daily/weekly inspirational email e-zines

I am a sponge. I get my hands on everything I can that is positive and moving.

There are many opportunities for learning right in your own backyard; you have to keep your eyes on the lookout though. Watch the Internet, newspapers, flyers around town, and listen for other positive people talking about prospective happenings.

Look for local seminars, business meetings, speakers, women's and men's groups, lunch meetings, service organizations, and networking events. Your workplace, local chamber, societies, and community organizations may even have speakers present. Plug into your network – there are many free or affordable opportunities to help you grow.

Also look for authors and speakers you really like who travel to national locations. If you're self-employed these opportunities can potentially serve as tax write-offs for you. If you're an employee, maybe your employer will send you to attend as part of your personal growth training or perhaps you can help bring the speaker to your place of work.

Personal growth is a big reason why I'm addicted to my network marketing company. There are many network marketing businesses to choose from.

I was introduced to this dynamic form of business while going to university. After being an independent consultant for a sensuality company for four years, I was living proof of how network marketing can influence your way of thinking. The business and personal development tools that were offered with this high-calibre company helped shape and develop my entrepreneurial mindset and dream big mentality.

After my success with the sensuality company, I switched gears and began sharing Swiss skin care and cosmetics as an independent consultant with a different home based business. Over the past four years, I have been sharing these high-quality products with my friends, family, anyone else who would listen (and even some who wouldn't)!

The real gift of the company I am part of now is the personal growth opportunities. I am blown away at every event, from local meetings to seminars to the national conferences; they are filled with exceptional, business-savvy, driven people who have been attracted to the opportunity and train their teams and sidelines generously. Motivational speakers are also hired to present and bring a different prospective to life.

Where else can you get training worth thousands of dollars for a small meeting fee or a reasonably priced conference registration? I'm not aware of another place. If you are, please let me know!

When I'm in a lousy mood and have had a horrible month of activity for my business or personal life, I go to an event for my network marketing company. When I'm in an amazing mood and my business is exploding, I also go to an event and I invite a guest to attend with me!

I challenge you to take advantage of every opportunity to invest in yourself.

• • •

Formal education will make you a living; self-education will make you a fortune.

~ Jim Rohn

• • •

Do you have a business, interest or hobby? I'm sure there is an event you can attend to be surrounded by like-minded people with rock-star ideas. Plug into a system that you can use as motivation to unleash your passion.

What's Holding you Back?

Do you have baggage or a past that is hanging over your head? Have you burned bridges in your life that cross your mind often or every once in awhile?

Start by reconstructing the relationship. Solve issues that are haunting you and deal with them face on. Find peace.

No one is perfect. Put the fault that created the tension behind you and become the bigger person. Get over yourself and make an attempt to apologize or find a resolution. If that isn't achieved, at least you attempted. You can cross that off the list that is haunting you and potentially holding you back from creating amazing relationships with new people.

This is a concept that is foreign in our society and seems to be one of the biggest obstacles in the lives of my friends and the many clients I have worked with as a life coach.

In a society where we thrive on gossip and rely on social media, it is very easy to dwell on negativity. Are you waiting for an apology from someone? I recommend you pull up your big girl / boy underwear and be the bigger person! As I suggested above, attempt to apologize or resolve, and then move on with your life.

• • •

Keeping score of old scores and
scars, getting even and one-upping,
always make you less than you are.

~ Malcolm Forbes

• • •

Stop talking about that person and wasting your precious energy thinking about how that individual did you wrong. Get over it – right now! If all else fails, hire a life coach and leap over this obstacle!

As Mufasa said in, *The Lion King*, "It's in the past, forget about it."

Personal Growth

I recently had a friend call and tell me her business wasn't moving forward. She didn't know why… blah, blah, blah. I was no longer actively listening. I had heard enough "negative" energy within the first statement and was biting my tongue.

I was thrilled when she gave me permission to talk and asked me, "What are you doing differently Robyn?"

I asked her one question, "What is the last book you read?"

She hesitated and responded, "Really sat down and read? Something in high school."

I knew that my friend needed to fill up her cup and learn, so the only piece of advice I gave her was to go to a book store or library and find a new book ASAP. It didn't matter if it was an inspirational, self-help, or business book. She just needed something to move her out of her comfort zone. Put down the *Shopaholic* and *Twilight* series. There is a time and place for those awesome books - *after* a fabulous motivational book.

There are a lot of different theories on "how much" reading will make a difference. My first personal coach taught me to read/ invest in myself for 90 minutes a day. The recipe I follow is 10 pages a day. That's it! You'll see it can be done in no time at all.

• • •

People often say motivation doesn't last. Well, neither does bathing that's why we recommend it daily.

~ Zig Ziglar

• • •

Read when you wake up laying in bed, taking a bath, eating breakfast, instead of watching TV, over your lunch break, having coffee, and when you are waiting for someone while sitting in your car. Be creative.

You can make time for anything you want – don't tell me you're too busy. If you are, then you're telling me you're too busy to become a more amazing person! I also make time to enjoy other methods of personal development. I listen to audio books while I drive to utilize that precious time, attend seminars, workshops, conferences – any opportunity to be in the presence of empowering, positive, uplifting people!

Remember, 10 pages a day. Try it for 21 days. That's only 3 weeks. I bet it will become a habit and you'll keep doing it at least a couple days a week!

• • •

First we make our habits, then our habits make us.

~ Charles C. Noble

• • •

Be Different

Be a doer, instead of a follower! Life isn't easy. Being in a good mood and leading by example isn't easy either. Anything in life – everything worthwhile – takes work!

Being a leader is the ability to embrace every bump in the road with integrity. When you're a leader, people look to you as a role model and observe how you react and tackle life.

We all have people who look up to us. You may not realize it but right now, someone is admiring you, whether it is one of your parents, children, partner, coworkers, and/or friends. Someone is watching you like a hawk. Lead by example.

• • •

A pint of example is worth more than a barrel full of advice.

~ Unknown

• • •

Something unexpected and drastic happened a few months ago that tested how much of a leader I was being. {Check out the before/after pictures on my blog www.robynbeazley.com for a chuckle!}

I went to the hair salon to get my hair colored and trimmed. The hairstylist was working on trimming the back of my hair and the next time I looked up I was shocked. The right side of my hair went from below my chin to above my ears in minutes. It was all supposed to stay at chin length! Oh wow! I immediately knew I was in for a big change. An attempt was made to salvage my hair. I stayed as calm as I could, but I was really upset.

I did not share where I got my hair done with my network. The stylist is human, the salon is a business, and both deserve to be respected. (Remember the Golden Rule, "do to others as you would have them do to you" Luke 6:31 NIV.)

As a business owner, I wouldn't want an upset client to ruin my name. I would much rather make it right with a form of compensation, an apology, and a show of appreciation for their feedback and support.

I embraced this drastic change because it's life! And if you know me, you know that I needed all the help I could get with a simple hairstyle to do daily.

[This unexpected change happened for a reason.]

Leadership is also about extracting the best out of people. I encourage you to empower others in your life by helping them realize their strengths and potential. Often all we crave is a pat on the back to ramp up our productivity and enthusiasm for a project. I often remind my husband that I'll work harder for praise than a raise. However, John often retorts with another favorite quote of ours:

• • •

Money isn't everything but it ranks right up there with oxygen.

~ Rita Davenport

• • •

Getting others to do what you want them to do, happily, is the real secret to being a strong leader. Combining all of the principles in this book should help you discover what other people are passionate about. This valuable information will provide you with ammunition to motivate them. When you're interacting with others you have the ability to dictate the mood of every conversation. Take a minute to think about that thought – let it sink in.

If someone called you and was in an "ugly" mood, it would immediately affect your attitude. Smile when you answer the phone. The person on the other end will hear it in your voice. Only answer the phone when you're in a good mood. Every interaction requires your full attention and positive attitude.

I spend a lot of time on my own, which I'm completely fine with, since my hubby travels a lot for work. This free time is when my creative, entrepreneurial, productive juices flow best. I spend many hours in my home office, which I'm in love with. The energy of the space is amazing and I get so much accomplished.

About a year ago, I got a mirror for my wall. I wanted to see myself while sitting at my desk. Time flies by when I'm working on the computer and I often need someone to hold me accountable. The mirror keeps an eye on me! I realize this sounds a bit creepy, but catching myself in the reflection wakes me up and gives me the impression that someone is watching.

If you walk into my office you might think it looks a bit strange hanging so low, but it's for me and no one else. When you spend as many hours tackling your entrepreneurial ideas as I do looking at the mirror at eye level, you will see that it's perfect! Plus, when the phone rings, I can look at myself in the mirror and make sure I'm smiling when I say hello!

Make the Best of Everything

After I took a leap of faith and experienced a big financial loss from a business venture, I needed to find a job to pay the bills.

After months of job searching at the start of the recession, I was offered a job at a local college. I instantly loved my coworkers and adjusted quickly to the routine of a regular day working for someone else.

Many family members and friends were surprised by how well I did since for a few years they had only known me as being a very independent, spontaneous, and self-employed young lady. The idea of me adhering to someone else's schedule was the joke and concern. My family and friends were shocked when I told them how much I was enjoying and embracing this new opportunity.

It took me nearly three months to even talk about this new "résumé builder" on my blog. Honestly, I was embarrassed by how it might make me look: an unsuccessful, entrepreneurial failure. Why would my network marketing team want to continue building a team with someone that had appeared to move backwards, and away, from their goals of working from home?

I don't recall when the turning point took place, but I finally snapped out of my negative attitude. My real friends would understand. Why did I really care what others thought about me? I have no idea. However, I'm glad I finally got over myself.

Hire a Life Coach

I am constantly developing new skills. Instead of referring to weaknesses I have, I simply describe a few skills as ones I still need to master.

Time management and follow-up have been known to fall through the cracks of my life, so I've been taking a new approach to focus on developing these two skills. I'm learning what having a routine is all about and prioritizing my commitments.

What do you need to learn? What skills would you like to improve?

I encourage you to look at every opportunity that comes your way as a chance to learn something. I discovered early in life that in order to be blessed with a chance to tackle new projects, you must be willing to learn something before you get the new opportunity.

You need to be prepared to constantly work on yourself. Our society is fast-paced and it's often challenging to schedule "me" time into the calendar. When is the last time you sat down to examine what you're doing in life and whether your work, hobbies, and friends are in line with your personal purpose in this world?

I first learned about life coaches two years ago when I signed up for a free coaching experience from an e-zine with a bestselling author. During my initial interview (to determine if I was a fit for the author's coaching program), I was moved by the evaluation process because it looked at every aspect of my life.

Long story short, my first coaching experience didn't develop or finish the way I expected. I was disappointed and didn't talk about this chapter of my life with anyone for a long time.

Luckily, I finally opened up about my exposure to a life coach with a close friend and was able to look beyond. I started working with a new life coach a couple months ago and my life has skyrocketed!

I work with my mentor on many different areas in my personal and professional life; on everything from my money management skills to focusing on my mission in life. If you have unachieved goals there is a good chance that an obstacle is blocking your path. We often need outside assistance to see a barrier, and then decide to either move it to the side or deal with it head on.

Another possibility is that you need to pinpoint your goal or identify the baby steps that must be taken before you can realize your dream. If you're climbing the mountain of life and come to a crossroads, get a second opinion instead of just flipping a coin!

My life coach is my accountability partner and helps me apply the laws of the Universe to my life. Working with a professional who helps me focus on my goals and dreams is so refreshing. I leave every session energized and ready to tackle the steps that are between me and the more outstanding woman, wife, daughter, friend that I strive to be. Coaching creates a clear picture of my current position and the steps to achieve new milestones in life.

I started being a life coach a couple of years ago (without the official title). Friends and friends of friends would contact me for inspiration or help overcoming the obstacles they were facing. I would invest my time to help them over the phone, through email, and in person. These experiences have encouraged me to become a life coach to more people. Having my clients share their "a-ha" moments is one of the most rewarding aspects of being in this profession.

If you are ready to move forward in your life, I highly suggest you explore working with a life coach. Every coach has strengths in different areas, with each one offering their own unique style of guidance. I encourage you to research and interview a few life coaches before you commit to working with one for a couple of months.

When you start working with a coach I urge you to invest at least three months with that person. You need to give the relationship time to develop and allow the coach to gain a deep understanding of your purpose in life.

Faith

I am a spiritual person, using prayer and time alone to reflect on life.

I wasn't raised going to church every Sunday (my family went a few times a year, especially on Christmas and Easter), and in junior high I started to explore faith more on my own. Then, in my final year of high school, my church hired a new minister. His foreign accent was so difficult to understand that I stopped attending. It was a challenging experience for me, because I didn't want to quit going to church. However, I chose not to explore other churches, as I was about to move away.

Immediately after graduating high school, I moved to Kansas where I attended college. I was a free spirit, a lost bird flying around, looking for a rest. After visiting numerous denominations and attending countless services with college friends, I just couldn't seem to find the right one for me.

It wasn't until my University years in Texas that I went to church on a Sunday morning with my friend (now husband) that my spirit was reignited. The energy I felt during that service through the pastor's message moved my spirituality journey forward.

I am telling you this bit of background information to remind you that in my opinion, you don't have to be raised in a church to be able to discover a spiritual leader right now. No matter your current state in matters of faith, I invite you to find a spiritual mentor, or many, to support you in your quest for personal growth.

Your spiritual devotions do not have to be in a church, they can be done wherever you are in your happy place: your home, in the park, on walks, sitting in a coffee shop, wherever you are. I talk to God daily because I know that everything I have comes from him and everything I do is for him. I also know that God has a plan, and as much as I want to know the answers now, I know everything happens when it's meant to happen.

You may be lost spiritually searching for a place to belong as I was - you may be asking yourself questions like:

- When am I going to meet the perfect partner?

- Why am I not married?

- When will I have a family?

- When will I get a raise?

- How am I supposed to reach a goal with an obstacle in the road?

- When is my break coming (I deserve it right)?

- Where should I be in my life?

On and on and on it goes…

STOP! You are the only person that can answer these questions. Once you eliminate the pressure of needing the answers to all of those questions right now, you start to live a more fulfilling and positive life.

Take the time to think about who and what you are attracting to your life. What are you saying, both to yourself and aloud?

Try saying, "Universe, I am attracting a new opportunity that will help me secure my financial future. It looks like this ____!" (Describe specifically) I discuss this in detail in the Dreams and Goals chapter.

One of my biggest suggestions for starting to build a strong foundation of faith is the book *The Secret* by Rhonda Byrne. I listened to the audio book and to this day have never read the physical copy of it or watched the movie.

As you can see, there are many different ways of absorbing the content of this book. A big thing my husband took from *The Secret* was to ask yourself the following question:

• • •

You are a magnet...what
are you attracting?
~ John Beazley

• • •

If you are thinking negative thoughts, that is what you will get. If you are thinking positive, that's what you will receive. One thing is for sure, you are attracting something whether you know it or not.

Faith is an experience of self-discovery. Take the time to learn everything you can. Surround yourself with spiritual people who will support your journey.

Amazing Action Steps

- Let go of excess baggage.

- Do what you've never done before.

- Lead by example.

- Stand behind your beliefs.

- Read 10 pages of an inspirational book each day.

- Invest in yourself by hiring a life coach or attending a conference for personal growth.

- Accept and adapt to change. It's not about someone changing; it's how you react to the change.

- Remember that you're always marketing yourself.

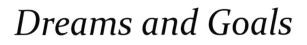

Dreams and Goals

• • •

*If you enjoy what you do, you will
never work another day in your life.*

~ Confucius

• • •

Vision

My dad is a visionary. Growing up he posted positive affirmations on the bathroom mirror and walls that he looked at every day. You know the ones that you could get from a truck stop that were on a laminated piece of paper? This was my earliest exposure to a version of a Dream Board or mantra to live by.

I copied the concept and started a collection on the back of my bedroom door. My first dream board consisted of four pictures. Three of the four images became mine within two years and the fourth another two years later. Here's what those four images were:

1. The logo for the Calgary Stampede Junior Livestock Scholarships, sponsored by BMO (a financial institute).

2. A red Chevrolet Cavalier.

3. The Dodge City Community College logo.

4. A house in a lush valley surrounded by mountains, with the word Montana included.

I went on to receive the agriculture scholarship two years in a row.

I was lucky to be given a truck as my first vehicle to drive. It was school bus yellow and had a headache rack attached. I could be seen and found anywhere in our small town. That truck was a wicked character builder. After driving "old yeller" for two years, my first car was a Cavalier. It happened to be green, but two years later, I got a red car!

I was offered the two-year scholarship to attend the college in Kansas that I wanted to attend.

My hubby grew up in a log house and moved to Montana to be closer to me during our courtship. Interesting how this image came true, differently than I planned. It just goes to show how unspecific I was.

Why We Dream(board) Together

This chapter is a collaborative effort between me, and my husband, John. We had fun creating our dream board together and enjoyed reliving the activity by sharing our different perspectives on the experience.

HE Said (John):

Have you ever wondered why some guys have all the luck? A beautiful woman, a great job, a big house, the time to go on vacations and getaways; it seems like they have it all. Just lucky right? What if you could discover a way to get what you want – anything at all?

Well, the first step to getting what you want is knowing what you want. A great way to help define exactly what you want is to create a dream board, which is a poster board or large piece of paper with images and words of your specific dreams, goals, and aspirations.

SHE Said (Robyn):

Dream boards can be whatever you want them to be. They can consist of pictures, cut outs, models, words or any images that you want. As Jack Canfield talks about in his book, *The Success Principles*, be specific. If you want to go on a vacation, then research resorts in the country you want to visit and find an image of the specific resort you plan to visit. Your mind doesn't know what you want; it just goes after what you visualize.

HE Said:

You should put the dream board in a place where you see it when you wake up and before you go to bed. I put mine on the mirror in our master bathroom – between my sink and my wife's sink. (Incidentally, we didn't share very well the first year of our marriage so a two-sink vanity was on our mental dream board before we built our house.) We put it on the bathroom mirror so we can both look at it while we get ready in the morning and before we go to bed at night.

The mind is a very powerful tool and will work toward these goals and thoughts even while you sleep. In his book, *Think and Grow Rich*, Napoleon Hill said, "If you can conceive it and believe it, you can achieve it." That book was written in 1937 and only came as a result of twenty years of research of the wealthiest men in the world. If it worked for the wealthiest men in the world, I figured what the heck; I could give it a try.

Believe it or not, I was excited to work on a dream board based on a few books that had promoted the idea. I told Robyn that I wanted to make a dream board and she was so excited to work on the project with me. It made a great date activity. We shared a lot of laughs and even scratched our heads at some of the things the other was cutting out to put on the board. And fellas, I also found out that this type of quality time is well rewarded.

SHE Said:

Anyone can make a dream board! I had the most fun creating my latest dream board with my husband and partner in life, John. This process allowed me to discover, more specifically, what John desires from life; and specific goals he wants to attain but hadn't openly communicated.

The first two dream boards I made for myself, I put in my office. However, our masterpiece dream board is pasted on the mirror in our master bathroom. We are able to look at it every day when we're home. Having our dream board in a shared space allows us to visualize our joint goals often and take actions that get us closer to achieving them – together.

In July 2009, while I was out of town, I received a call from my husband. "I want to make a dream board with you!" He said. My jaw dropped. Were my ears dirty? I was completely shocked. I had constantly dripped my positive energy and dream big mindset on him for over four years and did not see this coming at me.

This amazing desire hit me like a train. I was overwhelmed with emotion. I knew deep inside that I had been attracting this moment for three to five years. When you get married to your soul mate, everything is perfect the day you get hitched. Then reality sets in and you face challenges and bills. Life blinds your dreams when you least expect it. As a new wife, I constantly tried to keep our connection fresh and intellectual. John not only accepted, but also instigated the energy I was craving.

HE Said:

Only people who are serious about improving their current living conditions or achieving success should invest their time into creating a dream board. It can take as long or short as you want and should be specific. My wife and I spent about an hour going through magazines, cutting out pictures, and printing pictures from the Internet. The hardest part was actually sitting down and doing it. Once we started, we had a lot of fun and learned a few things about each other's dreams.

SHE Said:

I had to laugh because it seemed that everything John picked to put on our board was a material item, while I was selecting a lot of the things I wanted to experience. My husband spent hours looking on the Internet to find images of the exact items he plans to own: a private jet and custom motor coach, to name a few.

HE Said:

I put the logo for Rosetta Stone on my board because I wanted to learn Spanish. Being from Texas I had the basics down, but wanted to become fluent. As a result of my dream board, I now have Rosetta Stone [home study course] and I am still working to improve my Español.

SHE Said:

Examples of dreams that I included:

- A camera and the word photography, which represents my desire to enroll in a photography class.

- A picture of two babies, one wearing pink, the other blue.

- A written list of different goals that I didn't have images to represent yet.

- A woman (with her face cut out) wearing a gorgeous, red, strapless gown, which I plan to wear to the car presentation when our network marketing team promotes.

THEY Said:

Many of the items we included, we chose together. A picture of an Austin Stone style, bungalow home with an outdoor swimming pool represents our desire to have homes in both

Texas and Alberta. That way, we can travel back and forth to spend time with both of our families.

HE Said:

Just remember your mind is the only limiting factor – so dream big and be specific. Put it where you will see it daily, and most importantly, have fun with it. If you have a partner to share your life with, build your dream board together. This is a great way for guys to communicate what we are thinking, since we are not always the most eloquent in expressing our thoughts. Ladies back me up on this; women are not mind readers. As we learned early in our marriage, it is important for both of us to be on the same page and headed in the same direction (but that is another story in itself)! We can achieve more together than we ever could apart.

THEY Say:

If you know what you want and work towards it, you can dream your way to the good life.

Goals

Dream boards can help you see the bird's eye view of your life once you understand what direction you are headed. From there, you will need to explore your mission; and how to achieve the life you want to live, from a "big picture" point of view.

The summer after I graduated from University I moved back to Canada and lived with my parents for a while. I do a lot of my best thinking while I'm driving, but this time, I was in the tractor! We were preparing the fields for seeding and I found a small notepad in the cab of the tractor (my dad is famous for writing notes to remind himself of things).

That day I filled every page of that tiny notepad full of notes, while going round and round the field in the tractor. I titled this session *13 Things* and I wrote down 13 things I wanted to do. At the time, I wrote that my goal was for them all to take place between that day in the middle of May and the end of August. For the three and a half months following, I accomplished seven and a half of the 13 things (and continue to work on that list).

I realized afterwards that I didn't add the year behind my goal date. The list ranged from visiting 10 new states – to touching two oceans – to going through my clothes – to painting something!

After reflecting on this story and writing this chapter, I decided to make a new list of 13! That handwritten list is now in a frame on the wall of my office. It includes travel, career, and family goals.

Why 13 you ask? It's my lucky number! That's right, I'm opposite of many common superstitious characters in the world. However, I was born on April 13th and my parents wed on August 13th. (I know what you are thinking and they were married six years before I was born.) The number remains a favorite for me. I had considered titling this book with the number 13 in the title, but I concluded it might not be picked up and read by those concerned about the controversial number!

I challenge you to make a goal immediately!

Where Will You Be in 5 Years?

• • •

If you keep doing what you're doing right now, where will you be in 5 years?

~ Rita Davenport

• • •

I love this quote; it makes me think about the routine and/or rut I may be in. I first heard this thought provoking quote by the woman who coined the phrase, at a network marketing event. It has stuck with me ever since. Rita, ever so sincerely in her Tennessee accent, spears your heart with this quote, encouraging you to analyze your life carefully and to choose what you want to do tomorrow – the beginning of the rest of your life.

Whenever opportunities come my way, I think about this idea and it forces me to decide if it is going to take me a step up the staircase of life or down (backwards).

Life is a journey. I realize you have to experience the *Peaks and Valleys* (another favorite book of mine, and my husband's, by Spencer Johnson) in order to appreciate what you're blessed with.

Amazing Action Steps

- Cut out pictures and collect images of items for your dream board. If you have a partner, make a date out of this activity.

- When you write down your goals they are more likely to come true. What are your goals this month? Season? Year?

- Are you looking forward to something? If not, create, plan, or book something.

- Brainstorm creative places where you can find resources to help you achieve a goal.

- Remember that the accomplishment of many small baby steps helps you reach your big goals.

- Remind yourself that you can have and do anything that you set your mind to!

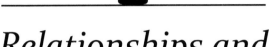

Relationships and Interactions

...

Don't put the key to your happiness in someone else's pocket – keep it in your own.

~ Unknown

...

Relationships

Live spontaneously!

I love keeping in touch with friends and family, through all communication mediums. I am an extrovert and a social butterfly.

• • •

You are the average of the five people you spend the most time with.

~ Jim Rohn

• • •

Early in my marriage, I was talking to my friends Sarah and Lisa, about holes in my communication with my new husband. They both highly recommended the book, *The 5 Love Languages* by Gary Chapman.

It totally changed my outlook on our relationship and explained a lot of things about the differences in our communication styles.

Whether you have a romantic partner or not, the same principles can be applied to any relationship you have. The book is a fun read and has an awesome quiz in the back to help determine your love language.

Get to know the people in your life. What makes them tick and gives them butterflies?

As an example, a couple of years ago my friend, Jessica, really wanted flowers for the romantic holiday, Valentine's Day. However, her man at the time made plans to take her for dinner. In his defense, it wasn't in his budget to do both. I quickly identified that her love language, for this occasion, was "gifts," and his was "quality time" or "act of service." Unfortunately, they were completely out of sync!

The key to an amazing relationship is effective communication: to discover what satisfies each other. After completing the quiz, I learned that I don't have just one love language, but a combination of three, none being what my hubby anticipated before the quiz!

Open and Optimistic

When I first told my dad about my boyfriend and now husband, John, he asked me two questions:

1. What are his grades? (We were in University)

2. Can he tell jokes?

Point of the story is that my father, who was 3000 kilometres away, didn't care what my new boyfriend looked like, where he was from, or what he wanted to do.

My wise father wanted to know if John was intelligent enough to challenge me and if he could make me laugh. Luckily, John passed the test, and I'm thrilled that my husband has a great relationship with my parents.

However, this isn't always the case. Not everyone is as open as my parents or as optimistic about life like my father. You have control over the attitude and respect you give your parents, siblings, and in-loves and this greatly affects the relationship that you and/or partner will have with your family. I encourage you to have an open and optimistic relationship with everyone in your life.

Avoid Judgment

I am far from perfect, but I have tried to eliminate all judgment from my soul.

• • •

If you judge people, you have
no time to love them.

~ Mother Theresa

• • •

This thought often comes to mind when I see a unique character as I'm driving through a city or walking into a store. I mentally slap myself, so I am reminded that I know nothing about that person's life, so I should stop trying to judge why they are dressed or acting like that.

I once obtained a contract where I was "warned" about one of the decision makers before interacting with this person. I ended up getting along famously with the individual. I was confident and invested time getting to know the person. I went into the contract with a clean slate and let the person show me their true colors. I put the judgment of the person that gave me this "heads up" to the side, allowing for my own impression and relationship to develop.

When you see unique individuals or situations, do you act like Simon Cowell? When he first got a glimpse of Susan Boyle on a United Kingdom reality talent show, his judgemental body language was transparent. Who is Susan Boyle? I encourage you to search www.YouTube.com for the video of her audition.

I was going into a grocery store one afternoon when it was pouring rain. I was hustling, but being cautious not to wipe out (I can be a bit of a klutz sometimes). Ahead of me, I observed a very "experienced" lady pushing her cart to a truck that was parked right outside the door. The full-size truck had something in the back with a tarp over it.

I observed the lady open the doors and lift her bags into the cab. My initial reaction was to wonder why on earth the driver was not getting out to help her. I put judgment aside and immediately went over to help her load the groceries.

I greeted her and suggested she get into the truck, I would load the remaining bags. She was so grateful. When I looked into the truck, a middle-aged gentleman was sitting in the driver's seat. It would have been easy to assume by his age and stature that he should have been out loading the groceries. However, when I looked in the bed of the truck, I could see that an electronic wheel chair was under the tarp. When I looked over at the man in the driver's seat again, I saw he at least one leg amputated.

The nice lady said, "Thank you so much. I hope someone will help you one day too!"

This random act of kindness made my day, week, and month – heck my year. I'm still reflecting on it. I'm not looking for a "good job" comment from you. I'm paying it forward in hopes you may read this and be on the lookout for an opportunity to help someone else!

Communication

We're becoming more and more reliant on emails and other forms of social media to communicate our thoughts. As a result, I believe that a lot of stress is generated from miscommunication and our misinterpretation of it.

As we briefly look back in history, one of the earliest methods of communication was mail. You'd write a letter and send it to your long-distance relatives and friends. It would literally take weeks to arrive. If the person wrote you back in a timely fashion, you'd receive a reply, weeks later.

Then, after our jump through the phone phase, we leaped to using computers. I personally "don't prefer" to write emails. I would much rather talk to you in person or in a phone conversation.

• • •

Communication is the response you get.

~ Dale Carnegie

• • •

John shared this brilliant quote with me after he read one of Dale Carnegie's books. I now think of this quote all the time. If I don't get the response I am attracting, then I instantly know that I didn't communicate effectively. I quickly attempt to recover and match the communication style of the person whom I'm corresponding with to change the result.

You've probably heard that a very high percent of communication is nonverbal. How you convey a message, is just as important and influential as what you say.

Invest or Let Go

Flush the dirty laundry. By this, I mean take out your relationship trash.

Are you overwhelmed with negative people in your life who you probably call friends?

You have two choices or you can combine them both into one action.

Leave these people behind and move on. Stop initiating conversation by phone or setting up dates to get together. Dramatically reduce the contact you have with these life suckers. You need this valuable time to get together and keep in touch with positive people.

Help these people subconsciously. You aren't a councillor, but if you feel that there is a pearl inside the oyster, then go above and beyond to bless them with your positive energy.

The reason I suggest the combination option is because you probably have people in your life that you need to wean away from, but it may be hard to identify who is an oyster until you step back. Often the negative people are family members, including your partner, whom you aren't able to completely sever from your life – ever!

Keep being an optimistic spirit in everyone's life. The individual with the ugly attitude has two choices. A) They can become more attracted to your optimistic personality or B) they will be moved into the friend of yours for a season (in the past) category. You always have the option to return them into your life emotionally for more seasons in the future.

If you feel there is a potential pearl inside the oyster, I encourage you to continue investing in the friendship. Your listening ears can make a huge difference in that person's life. Remember though, if you're giving 100% to a relationship, you must be getting 100% back over time.

I'm really lucky to have a huge network of friends. Everyone I have met entered my life for a reason. Many individuals are friendly acquaintances and others have become close friends. I have learned to protect my heart, as I don't want to be only one that calls, emails, and keeps in touch for very long. I love hearing what's going on in other people's lives, but I do love to be asked in return.

Are you getting value from your relationships?

People have commented to me over the years that I'm so lucky to have so many friends. I recognize how blessed I am to have such a large and wonderfully supportive network. My parents blessed me with opportunities to be involved in different activities, as well as the chance to travel and experience new places and cultures. I was also lucky to attend college and university in the United States. No matter where I went, either down the road or across the continent, I had to step out of my comfort zone and interact with others.

My network has grown because I ask questions of new people and take a genuine interest in them. I met some of my closet friends through friends and friends of friends.

Surround yourself with successful people and you're bound to connect with someone new that will help you realize your potential or unlock the door to your next dream!

Anything you do will come back to benefit you tenfold – I truly believe that!

Mentors

My parents are my rocks and have blessed me with a lifetime of insight and experiences to tackle the world.

As I mentioned earlier, my father is one of my biggest mentors. I have gained so much knowledge and wisdom from him, learning from his experiences and mistakes. To this day he is still known as Mr. Advice to me and many of our friends (whether we want advice or not, he gives it)!

My father is also an amazing listener.

• • •

We have two ears and one mouth, so that we can listen twice as much as we speak.

~ Epictetus

• • •

My mother is a true gift from heaven. Without going into much detail at this time, and not to freak you out, I'm convinced that my mom and I are "connected." I have learned priceless lessons from her: things like compassion, unconditional love, passion for travel, and an appreciation of nice things.

Many people I admire and look to for daily inspiration are my friends on Facebook and some have their own blogs and websites. I visit their web pages as often as I can for a dose of excitement. I am like a sponge and absorb their optimistic attitude.

I look up to a lot of people in my life and I try to spend as much time with those who are in my current network as often as I can.

My husband's grandmother, Nanny, writes the quote below on every note that she sends us as her signature. We have so much to learn from everyone around us, particularly the "experienced" people in our lives.

• • •

Smile, Stand Tall, Talk to God
~ Nanny

• • •

Lots of other mentors are still out of my arm's reach – for now! It is thought that everyone in the world is connected by six people; this theory is described as the six degrees of separation. I trust that with my connections, one day, I'll be able to narrow the six degrees and meet my mentors that aren't yet part of my first degree of separation.

Other amazing people I strive to be more like are in Heaven. I can only hope that a couple of them make up *The 5 People You Meet in Heaven,* an awesome, easy to read book by Mitch Albom.

Whatever you are aspiring to do in your life, attract the mentors to help you achieve it.

Amazing Action Steps

- Focus on improving at least one relationship in your life this year.

- Move on from negative relationships.

- Treat everyone with the same level of respect you would like to receive.

- If you don't have anything nice to say, don't say it at all.

- Make a conscious effort to ask people about themselves.

- Read the book *The 5 Love Languages* by Gary Chapman or get it just to do the quiz in the back.

- Plan a date night with your partner to connect and fall in love all over again.

- Treat your partner like you would your boss, Grandma, or someone that you respect highly and look up to.

- Make a coffee or lunch date with someone uplifting and love to be around.

- Write a thank you card or a just thinking about you note to brighten someone's day.

- Give experiences for gifts more than materialistic items.

- Be 100% present in conversations. When someone calls you or talks to you face-to-face, stop what you're doing and thinking – and focus on the dialogue.

- Smile when you answer the phone. The person on the other end will hear it in your voice.

- When you're communicating by email, if you're questioning whether or not to send it, hit "save draft" and sleep on it.

Live Inspired

These are my secrets to staying positive. They have gotten me to my current place in life. I look forward to seeing how the recipe changes in the next chapter of my life. Where you are in life is not as important as the direction you are heading.

Are you ready for change? Start today! Do one thing every day to live a more positive and empowering lifestyle. What does the next season of your life have in store for you?

YOU have to decide to re-launch your life! This recipe can only become the most divine dessert you've ever tasted when YOU make the first step towards a new, amazing YOU!

I leave you with a motto to live by... It stuck with me after reading it on a country decor sign in a store in Fredericksburg, Texas.

• • •

"Life should NOT be a journey to the grave with the intention of arriving safely in an attractive and well preserved body, but rather to skid in sideways, chocolate in one hand, margarita in the other, body thoroughly used up, totally worn out, and screaming, "WOO HOO, what a ride!"

~ Unknown

• • •

Live inspired,
Robyn Beazley

Resources

Personal growth and taking time for yourself are the most important investments you can make.

From highs to lows, I have learned to turn to motivational and self-help tools to inspire me and get back into my contagiously outgoing personality.

I would love for you to explore my constantly growing and changing list of recommended resources on my website: www.robynbeazley.com.

References

Books

Albom, Mitch. (2003). *The Five People You Meet in Heaven*. New York, NY: Hyperion.

Burg, Bob & Mann, John David. (2007). *The Go-Giver*. New York, NY: Penguin Group.

Byrne, Rhonda. (2006). *The Secret*. New York, NY: Atria Books/ Beyond Words Publishing.

Canfield, Jack. (2005). *The Success Principles*. New York, NY: HarperCollins Publishers.

Chapman, Gary. (2005). *The 5 Love Languages*. Chicago, IL: Northfield Publishing.

Hill, Napoleon. (1960). *Think and Grow Rich*. New York, NY: Crest Book, Fawcett Publications

Johnson, Spencer. (2009). *Peaks and Valleys*. New York, NY: Atria Books.

Kinsella, Sophie. (2005). *Confessions of a Shopaholic*. New York, NY: Dial Press Trade Paperback.

Meyer, Stephenie. (2006). *Twilight*. New York, NY: Little, Brown and Company Books for Young Readers.

Michelli, Joseph A. (2007). *The Starbucks Experience*. New York, NY: McGraw-Hill.

Movies

Hahn, D. (Producer), & Allers, R. & Minkoff, R. (Directors). (1994). *The Lion King*. United States: Walt Disney Pictures.

Miller, B., Miller, G. & Mitchell, D. (Producers), & Miller, G., Coleman, W. & Morris, J. (Directors). (2006). *Happy Feet*. United States: Warner Home Video.

Rudin, S. (Producer), & Dey, T. (Director). (2006). *Failure to Launch*.United States: Paramount.

Websites

thepioneerwoman.com   writewithdonna.com
victoriaosteen.com   youtube.com

Organizations

4-H   Toastmasters

Acknowledgments

Thanks to my editor and new friend **Megan Shapka**, for her priceless expertise as the Editor for my first book. From the day I shared my random thoughts and stories to the day the book went to print – you helped my dream become a reality. I will forever be grateful.

Thank you for the countless hours spent editing the content by my amazing friends, **Tiffany Dowell, Sheree Obbagy, Sandra Mills, and Randi Pierce**.

I am so blessed to be married to an amazing man and the greatest cheerleader, **John Beazley**. Thank you for encouraging me to achieve my goal to be a published author, for your patience as I spent countless hours working on it, and for your contribution to this book.

A huge thank you to my bestie **Laura Bodell** for inspiring me to start my blog (www.robynbeazley.com), which has developed into this book.

Thank you to **Donna Kozik** and her Write a Book in a Weekend Club group on Facebook (also visit www.WriteWithDonna.com).

Thanks Donna for encouraging aspiring authors to pursue their dreams.

I am grateful to every one of **you** for being a friend, follower, and reader. You've helped me become the woman that I am today and will be in the future.

About the Author

I was born and raised on a purebred cattle ranch in Alberta, Canada. Growing up, I was actively involved in 4-H and agricultural youth programs, showing, selling and judging livestock. Four years of post secondary school in Kansas and Texas later, I accomplished two dreams: earning a degree in Agriculture Business and meeting (and later marrying) the love of my life, my husband John.

Throughout my life, I have always been an entrepreneur, developing many businesses and contract positions that allow me the freedom to live my life as I dream. The challenges that entrepreneurship presents have further developed my strengths in networking, relationship building, professionalism, organization and communication. My mission is to focus on my gifts of empowering individuals to achieve balance in their lives through goal-setting, action steps and a positive outlook.

Many people I encounter ask me, "How are you always so positive Robyn?"

As far as I can recall, my journey to becoming an enthusiasm expert started in junior high. When I was growing up, my dad and I connected on a very spiritual level, and shared a vision on how to live life fully. In my eyes, my father was the ultimate optimist. My dad taught me to focus on the good. When the cattle market got rough, I remember him being the first in a conversation to respond, "Oh, it'll come back" or "The border will reopen soon."

From my observation, there was nothing that seemed unattainable to my father. I remember when my siblings and I were having challenges in school; he would encourage us to take a deeper look at the situation. Employing some creative thinking and positive energy, we were usually able to find a solution for most any challenge.

Dad taught us to talk about everything in life as if it had already happened in our favor. This helped me to build a strong belief in the "Law of Attraction," long before I ever heard that term used to describe a way of thinking. As I got older I began to see firsthand, the power of The Law of Attraction.

He also taught me at an early age to follow my dreams and provided me with opportunities to gain business knowledge. My parents gave me my first cow to start my own herd for my 9th birthday. When I was in junior high my dad gave me the opportunity to become a distributor to sell animal identification tags. These real-life, entrepreneurial practices helped me realize that the entire world was just a goal away.

In Grade 9, I became depressed and felt like I had no friends in school. Growing up on a purebred cattle ranch I spent many days travelling with my parents across Western Canada to showcase and market our livestock. We went to cattle shows, sales, and events that exposed me to a lot of culture and provided many experiences. I grew up fast and interacted with people of different generations.

I discovered the reason I was experiencing this loneliness was because I had a different maturity level than many of my school peers. Most of my true friendships and support systems were with students in higher grades, my 4-H circle, and friends from the cattle circuit.

I remember a day in Grade 11 when I went to a doctor's appointment, then decided I needed to take the rest of the day off. At sixteen years old, I was thinking that I needed to focus on myself. My soul needed energizing! I walked into a hair salon, in a small town north of where I lived, and got my hair colored professionally for the first time.

Feeling re-energized physically and more confident about my self-image, I got into my truck and just drove. My mind was spinning. I remember pulling over a couple of times to write down my thoughts in a journal that I always carried with me.

Finally, I ended up at a big box retailer in a city about an hour north of our ranch, where I bought my first three personal growth books. I don't remember the authors or titles, but I would recognize the bright, colourful, hardcover books if I saw them today.

I read through them and realized I was already living my life according to the ideas they presented. My earlier conclusion was reaffirmed; I was indeed a few years ahead of my classmates in my journey of life. Recognizing this helped me to start making the best of this chapter of my life as the young, strong, independent woman that I was, years ahead of my peers. Instead of trying to fit in, I started to focus on spending more time with the beautiful, growing network of people that surrounded me from other aspects of my life. I spent weekends, 4-H events, and vacations with friends from other towns that better suited me.

It was in high school that I learned you have to give up to go up. You must realize when a situation or atmosphere is holding you back, you either take action to settle for less than your best or strive for more. Look around the room you are in – if you are the smartest person there you need to find another room. There are several sayings, like birds of a feather flock together, but you are the average of the five people you spend the most time around. Recognize this and take action to be around who you want to be like – and don't be around who you don't want to be like.

In my final year of high school, my dad taught me to say, "You look good" to myself in the mirror every morning. This was my first exposure to self-talk and building my self-confidence.

Ever since then, I started to invest a lot of time in myself. I love spending time on my own, which may surprise you (if you know me)! I am an extrovert, but I crave alone time. I achieve it in many ways: reading a book, watching a movie curled up on the couch, and taking in the rays on my deck. I also love hanging out on the beach, beside pools and taking baths.

Driving is another way to enjoy my alone time. It's very enjoyable to me. I could drive for miles with no sound or the same song playing over and over and I wouldn't know. I love to get lost dreaming and scheming.

A few years ago, I drove from Alberta, Canada to Maryland, USA all by myself. I loved it. I went to see my boyfriend, John (who is now my husband), where he was training for work. Travel is one of my favorite hobbies and passions.

Although I am married, I am very independent. My husband travels a lot for his career, so we spend a lot of time apart. I use many of these occasions to refuel my "Robyn" time.

Publishing my first book as I move into a new chapter of my life is a dream come true. I look forward to adding motherhood to my resume in a few months and being blessed with the opportunity to share my time and energy with someone new.

More

Services

Robyn is keen to share the *Live an Amazing Life* energy with you, your team and/or organization as a:

- **Motivational Speaker**

- **Life Coach**

- **Consultant**

For more information, please contact Robyn through her website www.robynbeazley.com or by email at info@robynbeazley.com.

Share

Visit the *Live an Amazing Life* community and share your experiences at: www.liveanamazinglife.ca

Notes

Live an Amazing Life